Life Cycles

BAMBOO

Julie K. Lundgren

ROURKE
PUBLISHING

www.rourkepublishing.com

www.rourkepublishing.com

Photo credits: Cover © Benson HE, laurent dambies, Noah Bell, Reika; Title Page © T. Kimmeskamp; Table of Contents © worldswildlifewonders, Reika, Doctor Jools; Page 4 © Ilya Rabkin, ellakay; Page 5 © Hinochika, Brent Wong; Page 6 © worldswildlifewonders; Page 7 © Radu Razvan, 6493866629; Page 8 © Noah Bell ; Page 9 © Dirk Ercken; Page 10 © Reika; Page 11 © Le Do; Page 12 © Doctor Jools, wong yu liang; Page 13 © Losevsky Pavel; Page 14 © Benson HE; Page 15 © Reika; Page 16 © rehoboth foto, Noah Bell; Page 17 © SURABKY, Noah Bell; Page 18 © Noah Bell; Page 19 © cameilia; Page 20 © Bianda Ahmad Hisham; Page 21 © Torsten Lorenz; Page 22 © Mogens Engelund, Noah Bell, Reika, Doctor Jools

Project Assistance:
The author thanks teacher Dr. Xiaoqing Du and the team at Rourke and Blue Door Publishing.

Editor: Jeanne Sturm

Cover and page design by Nicola Stratford, bdpublishing.com

Library of Congress Cataloging-in-Publication Data

Lundgren, Julie K.
 Bamboo : life cycles / Julie K. Lundgren.
   p. cm.
 Includes bibliographical references and index.
 ISBN 978-1-61590-306-1 (Hard Cover) (alk. paper)
 ISBN 978-1-61590-545-4 (Soft Cover)
 1. Bamboo--Life cycles--Juvenile literature. I. Title.
 QK495.G74L85 2010
 584'.9--dc22
                                    2009047302

Rourke Publishing
Printed in the United States of America, North Mankato, Minnesota
033010
033010LP

www.rourkepublishing.com - rourke@rourkepublishing.com
Post Office Box 643328, Vero Beach, Florida 32964

Table of Contents

Giant Grasses

When you think of grass, do you picture a beautiful green lawn? Bamboo is also a kind of grass. These grass giants can grow as tall as trees and look more like a forest than a soccer field or yard.

Bamboos grow where winter temperatures are milder. More than 1,000 different kinds grow around the world.

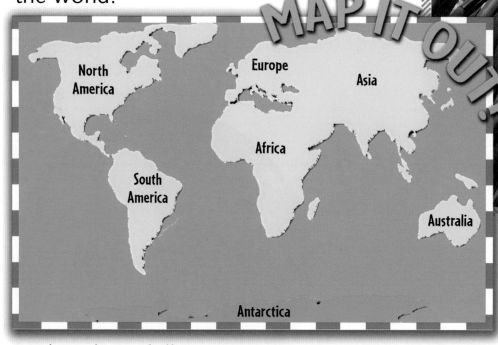

MAP IT OUT!

Bamboo plants of all sizes grow on every continent but Antarctica.

node

Leaves grow from the stem's nodes.

Like other grasses, bamboo stems have hollow centers and solid disks, or **nodes**, spaced along their length.

Giant pandas live in bamboo forests in China's mountains where they feed on bamboo.

Bamboo stems can make rich, beautiful flooring.

Compared to trees, bamboo stems weigh little and grow much more quickly. The nodes and tough fibers add strength. This makes bamboo very useful. People rely on bamboo to make houses, pipes, furniture, musical instruments, fences, cloth, and paper. Many animals depend on bamboo for food and homes.

DID YOU KNOW?

Some stores now sell soft, comfortable bamboo clothing, including socks and shirts.

Bamboo plants have roots, **rhizomes**, stems, and leaves. Rhizomes, or underground stems, store food for future growth. They also send out above ground stems and roots. Another name for an above ground bamboo stem is **culm**.

culm

node

leaves

rhizome

culm

roots

rhizome

Notice the new roots, rhizome, and a plump culm growing from the main rhizome.

roots

Roots take up water and deliver it to the leaves through the stem. Leaves turn sunlight into energy for the plant.

DID YOU KNOW?

Bamboo plants grow in different colors from tan to green to nearly black.

Bamboo Begins

Each living thing begins, grows, **reproduces**, and then dies. Scientists call this a life cycle. It happens again and again, like a spinning wheel that never stops.

The bamboo's life cycle begins with a sprout.

Millions of people enjoy the delicate flavor and crunch of bamboo sprouts.

DID YOU KNOW?

Not all kinds of bamboo sprouts can be eaten. Luckily, you can buy bamboo sprouts in cans, jars, and sometimes fresh from food stores. Why not try pickled bamboo?

Culms growing from rhizomes can reach their full height in one **growing season**. Some bamboos grow as much as 1 to 2 feet (30 to 60 centimeters) each day. Culms growing from seeds or under limited conditions may take years to reach full height.

Each culm comes up at its full width. As a bamboo plant ages, it sends up wider culms.

Bamboos grow best when they get water, sunlight, and nutrients.

DID YOU KNOW?

If you grew like some bamboo, you would reach your full adult height one to three months after your birth.

Bamboo stems can be stronger than trees.

Bamboo plants sprout new culms each year.

Bamboo culms have long, tough fibers that make them hard and strong. These fibers contain **silica** and **lignin**. Silica can be found in sand, glass, and cement. Woody plants, like trees, contain lignin in their trunks.

Keep On Growing

Two main groups of bamboo exist: running bamboo and clumping bamboo. Culms in both groups live only four to five years.

Running bamboos spread most often by sending out rhizomes, or runners, which sprout new stems. Running bamboos spread quickly and create a forest in a short time.

Gardeners more often plant clumping bamboos. Running bamboos tend to take over the garden or pop up where they are not wanted.

The rhizomes of clumping bamboo plants sprout much closer to the main plant and spread more slowly, with just a few new culms each year.

Flowers and Seeds

Many plants make flowers and seeds to reproduce. Though bamboo plants do not often spread by making seeds, they can. It takes a lot of energy for bamboos to flower and make seeds. It takes so much energy that bamboo plants usually die after flowering.

When bamboos flower, often all the bamboo plants in the forest flower at once. Most die after the flowers make seeds. The animals that depend on bamboos must move away or find something else to eat.

Ripe seeds fall to the ground. Those not eaten by birds or other animals make new plants.

Cycle Snapshot

Bamboo may live 30-100 years before flowering. Some will never flower at all.

DID YOU KNOW?

Bamboo leaves remain green all year—even those that are native to places with snowy winters.

Begin Again

Whether bamboo plants sprout from rhizomes or seeds, their ability to grow back quickly and easily makes them a **renewable resource**. In a world where people need to find ways to keep the Earth clean and healthy, they can harvest bamboo culms to make **green products**.

Bamboos harden over time. They are ready for harvest as timber in three to five years. Trees take at least forty years.

DID YOU KNOW?

Japanese gardens often have bamboos. Gardeners and visitors treasure them for their graceful stems and evergreen leaves, and as symbols of combined strength and beauty. In a Japanese garden, plant colors and textures mix with bridges, statues, waterfalls, and ponds to form pleasing scenes in all seasons.

Life Cycle Round-up

1 In the spring, culms sprout from rhizomes or seeds.

2 Culms come up at their full width. Rhizomes send up more shoots yearly.

3 Bamboo stems grow rapidly.

4 Rarely, bamboo plants flower and make seeds.

Glossary

culm (KUHLM): the stem of a bamboo plant or other grass

green products (GREEN PROD-uhkts): things made from materials that are friendly to the Earth, like plants

growing season (GROH-ing SEE-zuhn): the part of the year when rain and warmth allow plants to grow

lignin (LIG-nihn): a strong material found in woody plants like trees and bamboo

nodes (NOHDZ): short, solid sections in between the longer, hollow sections of bamboo stems

renewable resource (ree-NOO-uh-buhl REE-sors): something that can grow back or be recycled and used again

reproduces (ree-proh-DOOS-ehz): makes more of something

rhizomes (RYE-zohmz): underground stems that spread away from the main plant and send up shoots that start new plants

silica (SILL-uh-kah): a hard material that helps make bamboo stems strong

Index

Websites to Visit

www.americanbamboo.org/

www.biglearning.com/

www.exploringnature.org/

www.nationalzoo.si.edu/Animals/GiantPandas/

www.pbs.org/wgbh/nova/lostempires/china/miracle.html

www.urbanext.illinois.edu/gpe/index.html

About the Author

Julie K. Lundgren grew up near Lake Superior where she reveled in mucking about in the woods, picking berries, and expanding her rock collection. Her appetite for learning about nature led her to a degree in biology from the University of Minnesota. She currently lives in Minnesota with her husband and two sons.